4-15

D1205568

WITHDRAWN

APR 0 8 2015

Haunted Prisons

by Dinah Williams

Consultant: Paul F. Johnston, PhD
Washington, DC

Childrens Department
Menasha's Public Library
440 1st Street
Menasha, WI 54952

BEARPORT
PUBLISHING

New York, New York

Credits

Cover and Title Page, © Scott Griessel/fotolia.com, © Elnur/fotolia.com, © goodween123, and © sirylo/fotolia.com; 4–5, © Kim Jones; 6, © William Silver/Shutterstock; 7, © Albo/Shutterstock; 8, © Courtesy of Hargrett Rare Book and Manuscript Library/University of Georgia Libraries; 9, © Andersonville National Historic Site; 10, © Michael Criswell Photography; 11, © John LaVerne/Bulldog Tours; 12, © Carol M. Highsmith; 13T, © Bob Krist/Corbis; 13B, © Courtesy of Eastern State Penitentiary Historic Site; 14, © Idaho State Historical Society, photograph by Clay Almquist; 15, © Nagel Photography; 16, © M. Butterfield (Ireland)/Alamy; 17T, © Bettmann/CORBIS; 17B, © Nick Scott/Alamy; 18, © Andre Jenny Stock Connection Worldwide/Newscom; 19T, © ANCH/Shutterstock; 19B, © Michael S. Lewis/CORBIS; 20, © Bucchi Francesco/Shutterstock; 21T, © The Bridgeman Art Library; 21B, © Mary Evans Picture Library/Alamy; 22, © Travel Whimsy/Alamy; 23, © Jim West/Alamy; 24, © Heritage Image Partnership Ltd/Alamy; 25, © Stock Connection Blue/Alamy; 26, © Altrendo Travel; 27, © Moviestore collection Ltd/Alamy; 31L, © iStockphoto/Thinkstock; 31R, © Moldboard; 32, © iStockphoto/Thinkstock.

Publisher: Kenn Goin
Editorial Director: Adam Siegel
Creative Director: Spencer Brinker
Design: Dawn Beard Creative
Cover: Kim Jones
Photo Researcher: Picture Perfect Professionals, LLC

Library of Congress Cataloging-in-Publication Data in process at time of publication (2014)
Library of Congress Control Number: 2013041506
ISBN-13: 978-1-62724-089-5 (library binding)

Copyright © 2014 Bearport Publishing Company, Inc. All rights reserved. No part of this publication may be reproduced in whole or in part, stored in any retrieval system, or transmitted in any form or by any means, electronic, mechanical, photocopying, recording, or otherwise, without written permission from the publisher.

For more information, write to Bearport Publishing Company, Inc., 45 West 21st Street, Suite 3B, New York, New York 10010. Printed in the United States of America.

10 9 8 7 6 5 4 3 2 1

Contents

Haunted Prisons

Few sounds are as chilling as the metal bars of a prison cell slamming shut. Often, prisoners have been locked up in cells with murderers, thieves, and other criminals—sometimes for years, sometimes for life. Yet what about being locked up with a ghost? The **spirits** of many former prisoners—especially those who died while still behind bars—seem unable to rest in peace. As a result, they are reported to haunt jails and prisons around the world.

Within the 11 prisons in this book, you will meet many of these ghosts. Among them are a murderer who wore a white dress to her hanging, a ghostly black dog that follows **inmates** as they take their last steps on Earth, and a headless queen who leads curious visitors to her grave.

Death on the Rock

Alcatraz Federal Penitentiary, San Francisco, California
Opened 1934 • Closed 1963

On a bare, rocky island in the middle of San Francisco Bay sits Alcatraz Federal **Penitentiary**. It was built to house some of America's most dangerous criminals. No prisoner ever escaped from "The Rock," as this lonely and **remote** prison was called—some not even after death.

Alcatraz Federal Penitentiary

Alcatraz is one and a quarter miles (2 km) off the coast of California. The strong **currents** of the bay make getting to the prison by boat difficult—and getting out even harder. No one wanted to live there, especially the 300 prisoners who ended up calling it home. In addition to being cold and gray, the prison was very strict. For the first few years it was open, prisoners were barely allowed to talk.

As **convicts** stepped off the boat to the sound of the cold waves slapping against the rocky shore, the first thought many of them had was "How can I escape?" Thirty-six prisoners tried and failed, with thirteen of them dying in the attempt.

Three of those who died were shot to death by guards in 1946 during a bloody two-day shootout that came to be known as the Battle of Alcatraz. According to some, their ghosts have been felt at the prison since then. Decades later, in 1976, a security guard heard **eerie** cries and moans coming from the corridor where the prisoners died. When he checked, however, no one was there. Perhaps the prisoners' ghosts are still trying to escape.

The guards at Alcatraz were used to hearing stories about spirits that haunted the prison. For example, prisoners often spoke of seeing the ghost of a man from the 1800s. Most guards didn't believe the spooky tales, however.

A prison cell in Alcatraz

7

A Place Worse than War

Andersonville Prison, Andersonville, Georgia

Opened 1864 • Closed 1865

Andersonville Prison was run by the **Confederacy** for only 15 months during the **Civil War**. Yet in that short time, nearly 13,000 **Union soldiers** died there. With its terrible history, it's no surprise that Andersonville Prison is one of the most haunted places in America.

Andersonville Prison

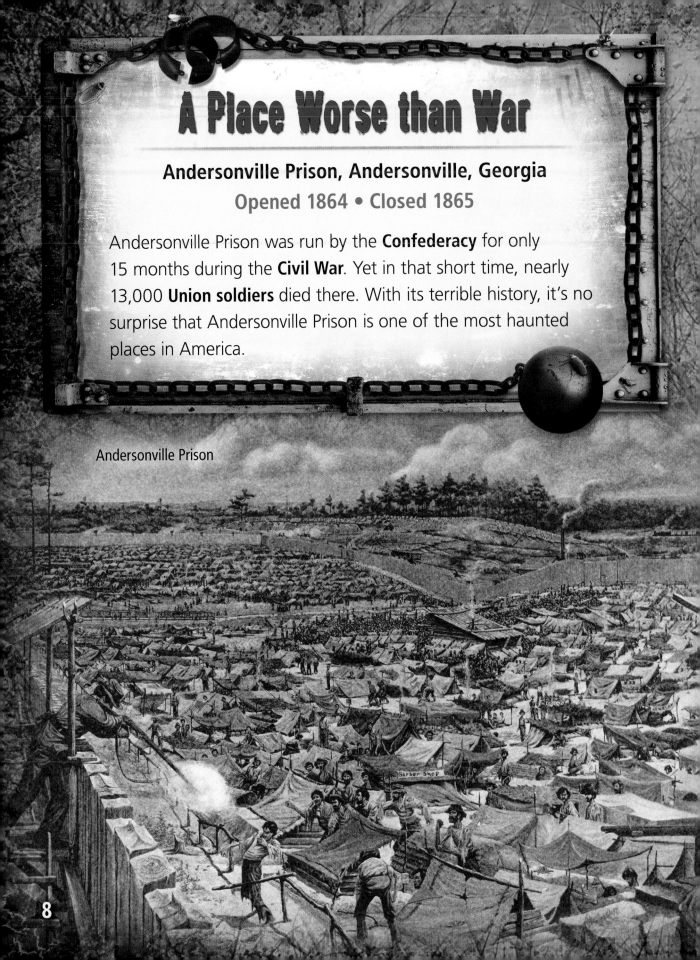

The first Union prisoners walked through the gates of Andersonville in late February 1864. By August, 33,000 men were crowded onto about 27 acres (11 hectares)—an area that had been meant for only 10,000. Many prisoners died every day from the heat, the cold, starvation, or disease. Many others were shot for simply getting too close to the fence that surrounded the **prisoner-of-war camp**. For those who survived, every day was a struggle. There was little food and shelter. A small creek that flowed through the prison was the only source of water.

Since the prison's closing, many visitors to the historic site claim to have heard the whispers and cries of men, along with the sound of gunfire. Others have smelled a terrible odor, like rotting flesh. In addition, shadowy figures have been seen in the fog. More than 140 years have gone by since the Civil War. Yet it seems that this area will never be free of its past.

After the war, Captain Henry Wirz, who was in charge of Andersonville, was arrested. He was convicted of war crimes for treating the prisoners so poorly. On November 10, 1865, he was hanged. Since then, there have been reports of his gray-uniformed ghost pacing near the prison's walls.

Prisoners at Andersonville

A Dangerous Hostess

Old City Jail, Charleston, South Carolina
Opened 1802 • Closed 1939

In its more than 100-year history, the Old City Jail housed a number of dangerous criminals. Thieves, killers, and even pirates were imprisoned there. Yet one person in particular stood out. According to **legend**, Lavinia Fisher was one of the most feared murderers in the early days of the United States.

Old City Jail

In the early 1800s, Lavinia Fisher and her husband John ran an **inn** outside of Charleston called the Six Mile Wayfarer House. The Fishers' small hotel turned out to be a very dangerous place. Some claim the couple poisoned men who stayed there in order to steal their money. Others say Lavinia was part of a gang that murdered travelers after robbing them.

Either way, Lavinia and John were finally caught and sentenced to death. On February 4, 1820, the couple was led out of the Old City Jail to be hanged. People say that Lavinia arrived at the **gallows** wearing a white gown that looked like a wedding dress.

Lavinia was buried in a graveyard near the place where she died. Years later, soldiers who were being kept prisoner in the Old City Jail during the Civil War claimed to see a woman in white pacing in a cell. Since then, others have seen Lavinia's ghostly face floating in the window of her former prison cell.

Why would Lavinia wear a wedding gown to her hanging? According to one version of the story, Lavinia knew that it was against the law to hang a married woman. Since her husband had already been hanged, she hoped that someone in the crowd would marry her on the spot—and save her life.

Inside the Old City Jail

Ghost of a Gangster

Eastern State Penitentiary, Philadelphia, Pennsylvania
Opened 1829 • Closed 1971

When it opened in 1829, Eastern State Penitentiary was considered a **marvel**. Its plumbing and heating systems were even better than those found at the White House. Still, after 142 years of use, it was time to abandon the building. Even then, however, the spirits of some inmates couldn't seem to stay away.

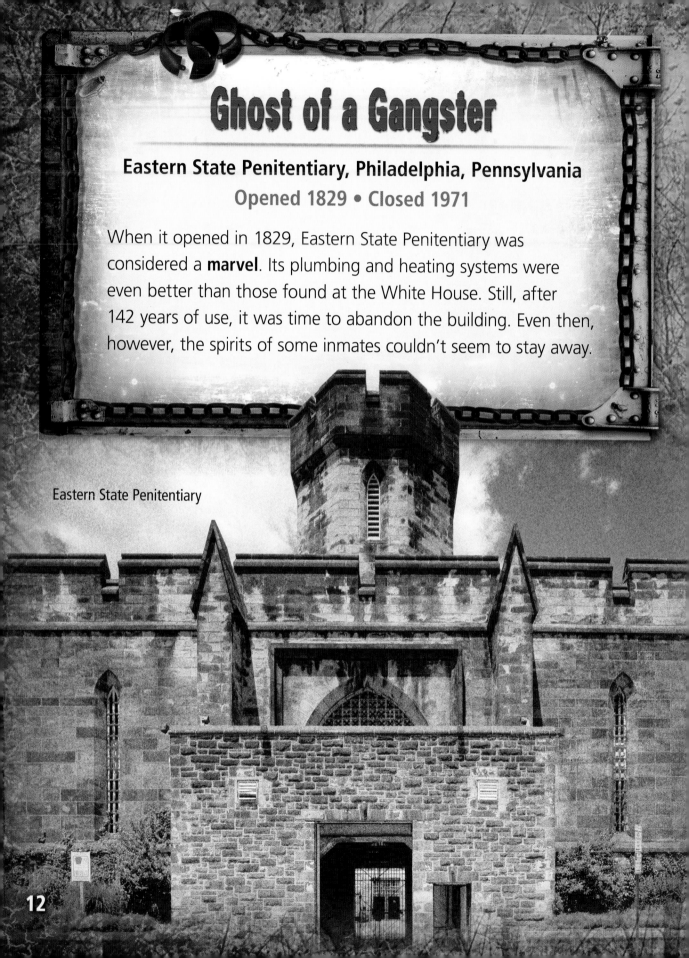

Eastern State Penitentiary

In 1929, Chicago **gangster** Al Capone was caught carrying hidden weapons. He was sentenced to eight months at Eastern State Penitentiary. Capone was so powerful, however, that he continued to run his illegal businesses from his richly decorated cell. Among the items in it were a polished wooden desk, paintings, and a radio.

Al Capone's cell

Yet even Capone had to follow some of the rules of the prison. He was alone so much that he became nervous and scared. At night, he screamed that he saw the ghost of James Clark—one of seven men Capone had ordered to be killed in a shooting that would later come to be known as the Valentine's Day **Massacre**.

Capone wasn't the only one to see ghosts. The prison is now a museum. Visitors have reported hearing the sound of footsteps in the cells as well as eerie laughter. One tower sometimes appears to have a shadowy guard still keeping watch over the empty prison.

In 1924, Pennsylvania Governor Gifford Pinchot sentenced a dog to serve time at Eastern State. What was the crime? The black Labrador, named Pep, supposedly killed the governor's wife's cat. In fact, however, the governor had visited a prison in Maine and had seen dogs being used to keep prisoners company and improve the quality of their lives. Afterward, he decided that the idea could work in Pennsylvania, too.

Pep

Last Man Hanging

Idaho State Penitentiary, Boise, Idaho

Opened 1872 • Closed 1973

Over the course of its history, Idaho State Penitentiary held more than 13,000 inmates. Although some managed to escape, most left the prison after serving their **sentences** and being released. A few inmates' **souls**, however, never broke free.

Idaho State Penitentiary

More than 100 prisoners passed through the front gates of the Idaho State Penitentiary and never left. They died in the prison due to old age, violence, or disease. Another ten were **executed** there, including Raymond Allen Snowden. Snowden was sentenced to death for murdering a woman named Cora Dean. On October 18, 1957, he became the last person to be hanged in the state of Idaho.

Today, Snowden's body lies in an unmarked grave in the prison cemetery. His spirit is said to haunt the grounds, which now include a prison museum. Snowden's ghost has also been seen many times in Cell House #5—the building where he spent the last days of his life. Doors there are said to lock and unlock on their own, and some visitors claim to have been shoved by an unseen force.

Inside Cell House #5

The host of a television show called *Ghost Adventures* spent the night in Cell House #5. He felt something very cold touching his arm and had someone quickly take a photo. In it, a dark shape is hovering above him. Could it be the ghost of Raymond Allen Snowden?

15

Firing Squad Hero

Kilmainham Gaol, Dublin, Ireland
Opened 1796 • Closed 1924

When people walk through the largest empty prison in Ireland, their footsteps echo in the **vacant** halls. Yet for more than a hundred years, this jail was packed with prisoners. Many were executed for their crimes. In a way, however, some lived on. They would later be hailed as heroes who changed Ireland's history.

Kilmainham Gaol

In 1796, Kilmainham **Gaol** began holding prisoners guilty of everything from murder to simply begging on the street. For many years, until 1881, men, women, and children were imprisoned together. Up to five people were packed into each cold, dark cell.

In April 1916, about 2,000 Irish citizens **rebelled** against the British rule of their country and the harsh conditions that came along with it. Hundreds were arrested and imprisoned in the jail. In May, 14 of the rebellion's leaders were executed there by firing squad. The last to die was James Connolly, who had been badly injured during the rebellion in April. His brave struggle for Irish independence made him a hero to many in Ireland.

James Connolly

In the 1960s, Kilmainham Gaol was turned into a museum. Since then, workers at the museum have noticed odd things, such as strange cold spots and mysterious footsteps. These staff members are not alone in their uneasiness. Visiting schoolchildren refused to enter the building, claiming to see spirits roaming the halls.

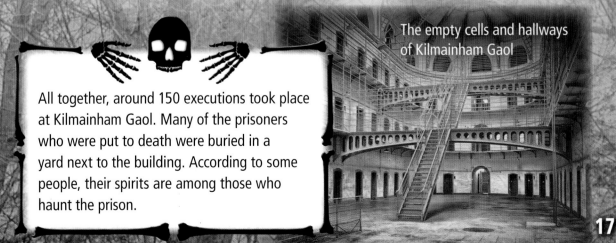

The empty cells and hallways of Kilmainham Gaol

All together, around 150 executions took place at Kilmainham Gaol. Many of the prisoners who were put to death were buried in a yard next to the building. According to some people, their spirits are among those who haunt the prison.

The Death House

Wyoming Frontier Prison, Laramie, Wyoming
Opened 1901 • Closed 1981

Prisons are designed to be harsh places. Living in one is supposed to be a punishment. Yet even among prisons, few places were as grim as Wyoming Frontier Prison. Today, at least one ghost seems determined to keep things gloomy.

Wyoming
Frontier Prison

When Wyoming Frontier Prison opened in 1901, its 104 dark, cramped cells had no electricity or running water, and little heat. **Breakouts** by prisoners were fairly common. During two days in 1912, nearly 30 inmates escaped through the prison's wooden walls. Although stone walls were later built, some prisoners still managed to break out. In 1927, five inmates got away by sawing through the bars of a window. Two others used a can opener to dig an escape route to the roof.

An old-fashioned can opener

The only other way for prisoners to escape was by dying. In 1916, a separate section of the prison, known as the "death house," was built with cells for prisoners on **death row**. In 1965, Andrew Pixley became the last man to be executed at the prison.

Forty-four years later, in 2009, a team of ghost hunters visited Wyoming Frontier Prison. They said an angry male spirit, possibly Andrew Pixley, still haunts the death house. They also recorded the sound of footsteps that occurred there, even though no one was around.

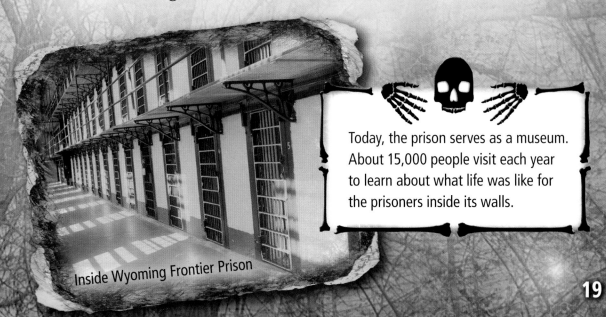

Inside Wyoming Frontier Prison

Today, the prison serves as a museum. About 15,000 people visit each year to learn about what life was like for the prisoners inside its walls.

A Headless Queen

Tower of London, London, England

Opened 1097 • Closed 1952

Nearly 1,000 years ago, the Tower of London was built as a castle by a powerful king named William the Conqueror. During its long history, important people were imprisoned there. The Tower was also the site of several **beheadings**. No wonder so many headless ghosts have been seen there!

Tower of London

During the 1500s, an English lady named Anne Boleyn stayed in the Tower of London twice. First, in 1533, she spent the night there as an honored guest before becoming King Henry VIII's second wife and queen. Then, in 1536, she was back for a very different reason. King Henry—who wanted to get rid of her in order to marry another woman—had her imprisoned in the Tower for **treason** and other crimes.

Anne Boleyn imprisoned in the Tower of London

Soon after, Anne was sentenced to death by beheading. On May 19, 1536, she spoke her final words to a crowd that had gathered to witness her execution in the Tower's courtyard. Minutes later a swordsman cut off her head with a single stroke.

Since her death, Anne Boleyn's headless ghost has been seen numerous times throughout the Tower. She has even led people to her grave. In 1864, one guard tried to stop her spirit with his **bayonet**. He claimed to have received a shock so strong that it knocked him out.

Former prisoners are not the only spirits haunting the Tower. Legend has it that in 1816, a huge ghostly bear appeared in a doorway. The sight scared a guard so badly that he died from fear. Some people say the strange beast was the ghost of the polar bear that had lived in a zoo that had been kept on the grounds.

The zoo at the Tower of London

Dead But Not Gone

West Virginia State Penitentiary, Moundsville, West Virginia
Opened 1876 • Closed 1995

West Virginia State Penitentiary was built to house only 480 people. By the 1930s, it had more than four times that many. Riots, fires, and executions occurred during the prison's history. Now that it is closed, ghosts, instead of prisoners, pack the dark corridors.

West Virginia State Penitentiary

The overcrowded West Virginia State Penitentiary loomed like a stone castle. Three prisoners lived in each tiny 5 x 7 foot (1.5 x 2.1 m) cell that was meant to hold just one person at a time. The only inmates who were not packed together were those on death row. Between 1899 and 1959, nearly 100 men were put to death. Many of the executions occurred in an area called North Wagon Gate. Now it's the place where restless spirits have been sighted. Some visitors have even reported hearing ghosts and being touched by them as well.

Another area that has seen ghostly activity is the Wheel House. This revolving door with iron bars instead of glass panels separated the **warden** from the inmates. While no prisoners have entered the prison for years, some say that unseen forces still cause the door to turn.

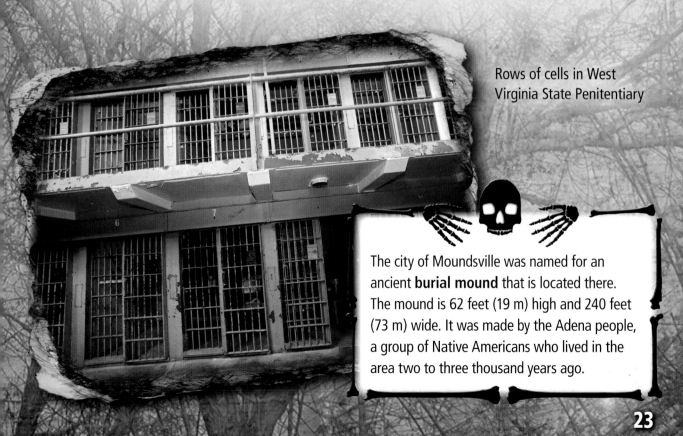

Rows of cells in West Virginia State Penitentiary

The city of Moundsville was named for an ancient **burial mound** that is located there. The mound is 62 feet (19 m) high and 240 feet (73 m) wide. It was made by the Adena people, a group of Native Americans who lived in the area two to three thousand years ago.

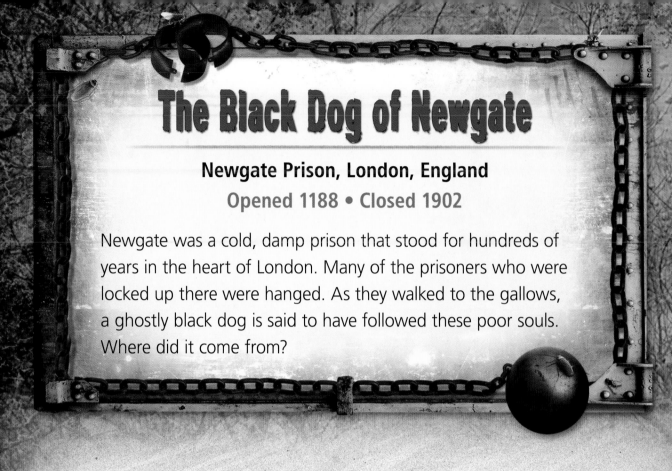

The Black Dog of Newgate

Newgate Prison, London, England
Opened 1188 • Closed 1902

Newgate was a cold, damp prison that stood for hundreds of years in the heart of London. Many of the prisoners who were locked up there were hanged. As they walked to the gallows, a ghostly black dog is said to have followed these poor souls. Where did it come from?

Newgate Prison

People have told different stories to explain the black dog seen at Newgate. The most famous—and most horrifying—comes from a short book that was written in the 1590s by a prisoner named Luke Hutton.

Hutton's tale, *The Black Dog of Newgate*, is set 300 years earlier, when the people of London were suffering from a **famine**. According to the story, a **scholar** was sent to the prison during this time for practicing **sorcery**. There, he was killed and eaten by starving inmates. Soon after, a ghostly black dog appeared—as if it had been sent by the murdered man to haunt the prison. From then on, the dog arrived at every execution. It would move alongside the **condemned** prisoner down "Deadman's Walk." This passageway led to the gallows and the cemetery where the dead prisoners were often buried.

Today, hundreds of years after the events in Hutton's tale, the prison is gone. However, the passageway still exists. A ghostly dark shadow is occasionally seen moving by the ivy-covered wall, along with the sound of dragging footsteps.

Hutton described the black dog as having glowing yellow eyes and breath that looked like smoke as it came out of its nostrils.

The Warden and His Wife

Ohio State Reformatory, Mansfield, Ohio
Opened 1896 • Closed 1990

Ohio State Reformatory has one of the largest **cell blocks** in the world. With six hundred cells lining its six floors, the building looks like a beehive. More than 155,000 inmates were locked up there over the years. Yet it is a prison warden and his wife, and not any of the thousands of prisoners, who are its most famous ghosts.

Ohio State Reformatory

In 1950, Arthur Glattke was the warden of Ohio State Reformatory. Like previous wardens and their families, Arthur and his wife Helen lived in a house behind the prison. There, one day in November, Helen was searching in a closet for a jewelry box. Suddenly, a loaded pistol fell from the closet shelf. The gun went off, killing her. A little over nine years later, Arthur suffered a fatal heart attack in his office.

Today, the ghosts of both Arthur and Helen Glattke are said to haunt the reformatory. Visitors to the prison museum claim to hear the faint sound of the warden and his wife talking. Others have smelled the scent of roses, which Helen loved, in the home's pink bathroom.

Besides the sightings of the warden and his wife, other ghostly signs have appeared at the prison. In one cell, visitors have heard the sound of running and a cell door slamming shut. There have also been reports of people in empty rooms being pushed, hearing voices and footsteps, and seeing strange shadows.

In 1993, the movie *The Shawshank Redemption*, based on a story by the famous horror writer Stephen King, was filmed at the reformatory. The film's popularity may have saved the prison from being torn down. People started visiting the prison to see what it really looked like, and today there are Shawshank tours.

TIM ROBBINS MORGAN FREEMAN

THE
SHAWSHANK
REDEMPTION

Fear can hold
you prisoner...   ...Hope can set
you free

A poster for the film *The Shawshank Redemption*

Haunted Prisons

Ohio State Reformatory
Mansfield, Ohio

Visitors still hear the conversations of a couple who lived and died here more than fifty years ago.

West Virginia State Penitentiary
Moundsville, West Virginia

Ghosts continue to turn a revolving door in an abandoned prison.

Alcatraz Federal Penitentiary
San Francisco, California

Prisoners never escaped from "The Rock," some not even in death.

Eastern State Penitentiary
Philadelphia, Pennsylvania

Gangster Al Capone saw ghosts while serving time here.

Idaho State Penitentiary
Boise, Idaho

The spirit of a man hanged for murder can't break free.

Old City Jail
Charleston, South Carolina

A woman who wore a white dress to her execution is still seen here.

Andersonville Prison
Andersonville, Georgia

The ghosts of mistreated soldiers haunt a Civil War prison.

Wyoming Frontier Prison
Laramie, Wyoming

A section called the "death house" is haunted by the last man who was executed there.

NORTH AMERICA

SOUTH AMERICA

Atlantic Ocean

Pacific Ocean

Around the World

Kilmainham Gaol
Dublin, Ireland

An old prison is still home to the souls of Irish freedom fighters.

Tower of London
London, England

The headless ghost of a queen greets visitors at this famous prison.

Newgate Prison
London, England

A ghostly black dog follows prisoners to their executions.

Arctic Ocean

EUROPE

ASIA

AFRICA

Indian Ocean

AUSTRALIA

Southern Ocean

ANTARCTICA

Glossary

bayonet (BAY-uh-net) a long knife that is fastened to the end of a rifle

beheadings (bi-HED-ings) executions in which people's heads are chopped off

breakouts (BRAKE-outs) escapes

burial mound (BER-ee-uhl MOUND) a raised area of land where dead bodies are buried

cell blocks (SELL BLOKS) groups of prison cells

Civil War (SIV-il WOR) the U.S. war between the Southern states and the Northern states, which lasted from 1861–1865

condemned (kuhn-DEMD) judged guilty of a crime

Confederacy (*kuhn*-FED-ur-uh-see) the group of 11 U.S. Southern states that fought the North during the U.S. Civil War (1861–1865)

convicts (KON-vikts) people found guilty of crimes who are serving time in prison

currents (KUR-uhnts) the movement of water in an ocean or river

death row (DETH ROW) an area of a prison where prisoners who are sentenced to die stay until the time of their execution

eerie (EER-ee) spooky

executed (EK-suh-*kyoo*-tid) put to death

famine (FAM-un) a shortage of food

gallows (GAL-ohz) a wooden frame used to hang criminals

gangster (GANG-stur) someone who is part of a group of criminals

gaol (JAYL) the spelling of *jail* in England and Ireland

inmates (IN-mayts) prisoners

inn (IN) a small hotel

legend (LEJ-uhnd) a story handed down from the past that may be based on fact but is not always completely true

marvel (MAR-vuhl) something extraordinary; a wonder

massacre (MAS-uh-*kur*) the killing of a large number of people

penitentiary (*pen*-uh-TEN-shuh-ree) a prison, usually a state or federal prison

prisoner-of-war camp (PRIZ-uhn-ur-UHV-WOR KAMP) a place where soldiers captured during wartime are held and guarded by the enemy

rebelled (rih-BELD) fought against those in power

remote (ri-MOHT) difficult to reach

scholar (SKOL-ur) a person who studies one or more subjects and knows a lot about them

sentences (SEN-tuhn-suhz) periods of time people have to spend in jail as punishment for a crime

sorcery (SAWR-suhr-ee) magic that is done with the help of evil spirits; witchcraft

souls (SOHLZ) the spirits of people who have died

spirits (SPIHR-its) supernatural creatures, such as ghosts

treason (TREE-zuhn) the crime of betraying one's country

Union soldiers (YOON-yuhn SOHL-jurz) soldiers who fought for the North during the U.S. Civil War (1861–1865)

vacant (VAY-kuhnt) empty

warden (WAR-duhn) a person in charge of a prison

Bibliography

Austin, Joanne. *Weird Hauntings: True Tales of Ghostly Places.* New York: Sterling (2006).

Davis, Jamie. *Haunted Asylums, Prisons, and Sanatoriums.* Woodbury, MN: Llewellyn Publications (2013).

Hauck, Dennis William. *Haunted Places: The National Directory.* New York: Penguin Books (2002).

Holzer, Hans. *Ghosts: True Encounters with the World Beyond.* New York: Black Dog & Leventhal (2005).

Read More

Hamilton, John. *Haunted Places (The World of Horror).* Edina, MN: ABDO (2007).

Hawes, Jason, and Grant Wilson. *Ghost Hunt: Chilling Tales of the Unknown.* New York: Little, Brown and Company (2010).

Teitelbaum, Michael. *Ghosts and Real-Life Ghost Hunters.* New York: Scholastic (2008).

Williams, Dinah. *Abandoned Insane Asylums (Scary Places).* New York: Bearport (2008).

Learn More Online

To learn more about haunted prisons, visit
www.bearportpublishing.com/ScaryPlaces

Index

About the Author

Dinah Williams is an editor and children's book author. Her books include *Shocking Seafood; Slithery, Slimy, Scaly Treats; Monstrous Morgues of the Past; Haunted Houses;* and *Spooky Cemeteries*, which won the Children's Choice Award. She lives in Cranford, New Jersey.

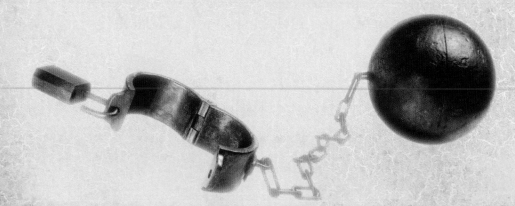